MARY COHEN
DANCE DUETS

© 2001 by Faber Music Ltd
First published in 2001 by Faber Music Ltd
3 Queen Square London WC1N 3AU
Music processed by Mary Cohen
Übersetzung Dorothee Göbel
Cover illustration by John Levers
Printed in England by Caligraving Ltd
All rights reserved

ISBN 0-571-52082-0

To buy Faber Music publications or to find out about the full range of titles available
please contact your local music retailer or Faber Music sales enquiries:

Faber Music Limited, Burnt Mill, Elizabeth Way, Harlow, CM20 2HX England
Tel: +44 (0)1279 82 89 82   Fax: +44 (0)1279 82 89 83
sales@fabermusic.com   www.fabermusic.com

DANCE DUETS

MARY COHEN

1 Polka

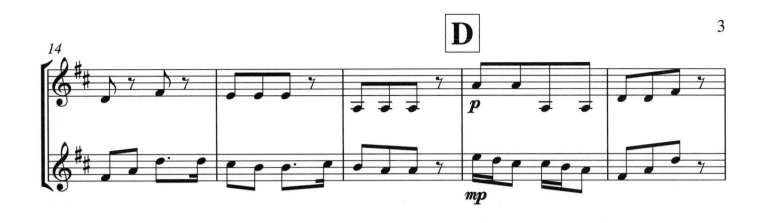

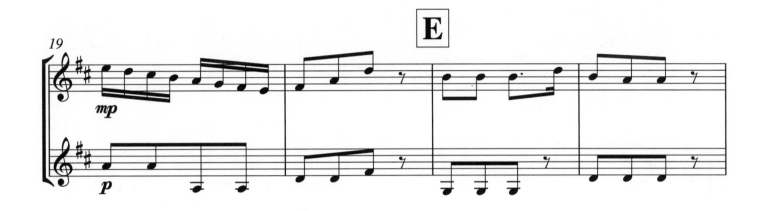

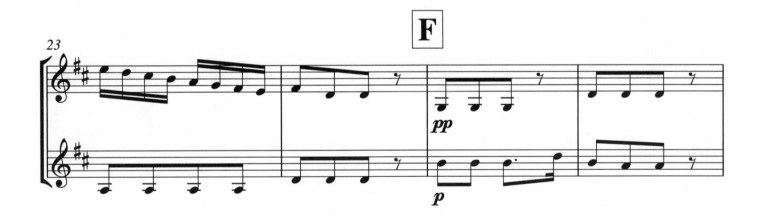

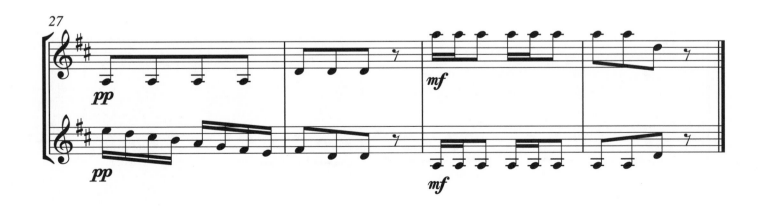

4

2 Tarantella

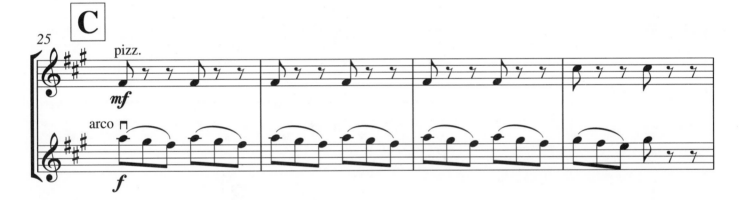

Da Capo al ⊕ poi al Coda

⊕ *CODA*

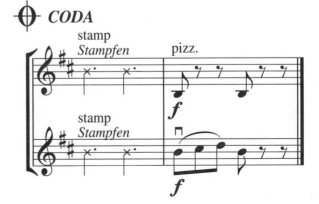

3 Rumba

8

4 Waltz

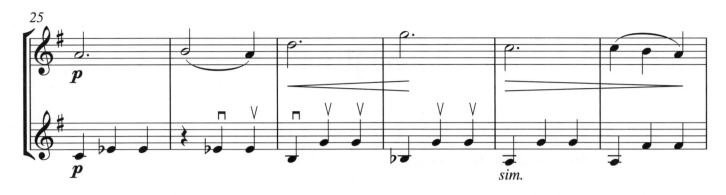

C

D

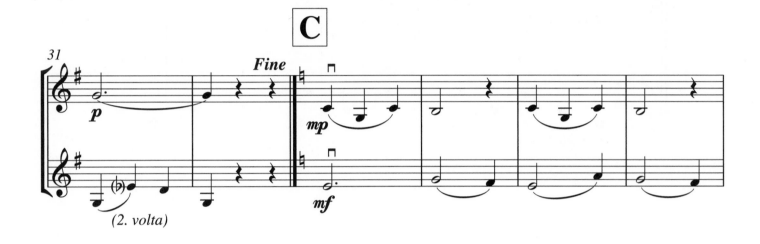

5 Ragtime

Dal Segno al ⊕ poi al Coda

6 Saltarello

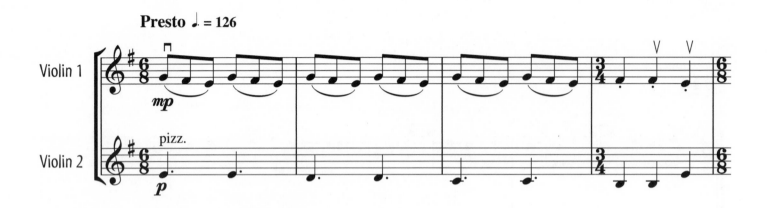

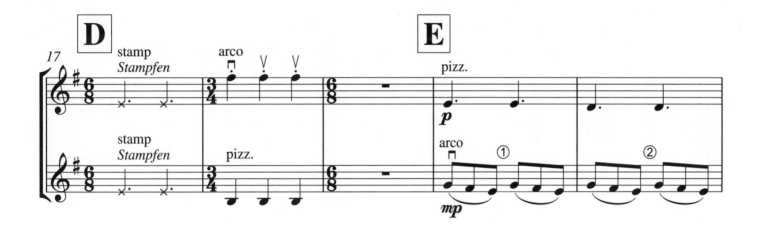

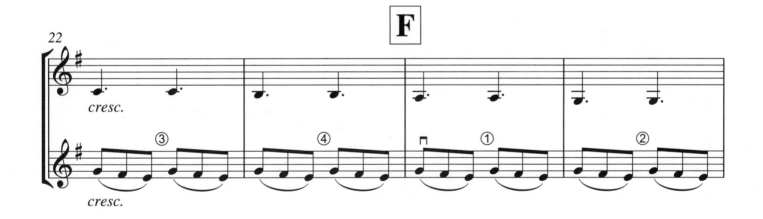

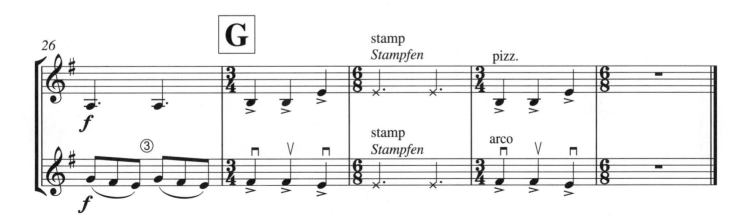

7 Hoedown

PERFORMANCE NOTES

Polka

The Polka is a dance from Eastern Europe that comes in several versions. This one has a heel-to-toe 'click' at the end of the 2nd and 3rd bars. Practise clapping the rhythm first; be sure to stay together precisely and keep a steady beat.

Tarantella

A lively Italian dance, taking its name from the town of Taranto. Think 'two in a bar' and keep a steady pulse. Watch out for the ultra quick changes from arco to pizzicato and back.

Rumba

This dance has its origins in Cuba. Both players should think in quavers all the way through, so Violin 1: make sure your tune fits 3+3+2 exactly. Violin 2: if your pizzicato finger gets tired, try playing your violin 'banjo style', plucking with your thumb. Have a go at swapping parts too.

Waltz

Waltzes sound best when you create a 'one in a bar' feel. Take great care with the accompanying figures. Violin 2: bars 1–32, give the 1st beat a slight emphasis and make the 2nd and 3rd beats lighter, but without exaggerating.

Ragtime

The most famous ragtime composer was an American, Scott Joplin, who said that ragtimes should never be played quickly. Work at getting a light, leggiero stroke without it becoming too staccato; the bow needs to travel a long way in a short time, using very little arm weight. Playing near the fingerboard will help.

Saltarello

A catchy 16th-century Italian dance (literally a 'little hop') with a fast-moving figure against a ground bass. The $6/8$ bars prepare for the hop in the $3/4$ bar. ♪ = ♪, so keep the pulse the same throughout and the $3/4$ bars will sound rather jazzy with three beats in the time of two.

Hoedown

This is an American square dance. Play the double-stopping confidently, placing your bow on an imaginary in-between string. The syncopated rhythm is easy if you think 'two in a bar'. Both players could stamp on the accented notes in bars 10, 12 and so on.

HINWEISE ZUR AUFFÜHRUNG

Polka

Die Polka stammt aus Osteuropa; es gibt sie in verschiedenen Varianten. Die vorliegende Polka verlangt einen „Klick" Ferse-Spitze am Schluß des zweiten und dritten Takts. Den Rhythmus zuerst klatschen; auf genaues Zusammenspiel und gleichmässiges Tempo achten.

Tarantella

Ein lebhafter italienischer Tanz, dessen Name sich von der Stadt Tarent herleitet. Zwei Zählzeiten pro Takt denken und den lebhaften Grundrhythmus gleichmässig beibehalten. Aufpassen bei den besonders schnellen Wechseln von arco zu pizzicato und zurück.

Rumba

Dieser Tanz stammt aus Kuba. Beide Spieler sollten durchgehend auf Achtel zählen. Violine I: dabei genau auf die 3+3+2 achten. Violine II: Sollte der Pizzicato-Finger ermüden, kann man probieren, die Violine wie ein Banjo zu spielen, also mit dem Daumen zupfen. Wechselt auch mal die Stimmen!

Walzer

Walzer klingen am besten, wenn man ganztaktig denkt. Die Begleitfiguren sorgfältig spielen. Violine II in Takten 1–32: Die erste Zählzeit im Takt leicht betonen, die zweite und dritte Zählzeit leichter spielen – aber nicht übertreiben!

Ragtime

Der berühmteste Komponist von Ragtimes war der Amerikaner Scott Joplin. Er sagte, dass Ragtimes nie schnell gespielt werden sollten. Bemüht euch um ein leichtes Détaché, ohne zu sehr in die Nähe eines Staccato zu kommen. Der Bogen muss in kurzer Zeit einen langen Weg zurücklegen, dabei wenig Gewicht vom Arm einsetzen. Einfacher ist das, wenn man in der Nähe des Griffbretts streicht.

Saltarello

Ein beliebter italienischer Tanz aus dem 16. Jahrhundert (wörtlich übersetzt „ein kleiner Sprung") mit einer schnellen Spielfigur über einem durchlaufenden Bass. Die $6/8$-Takte bereiten auf den Sprung im $3/4$-Takt vor. ♪ = ♪, das Metrum also beibehalten; dann werden die $3/4$-Takte mit ihren drei Zählzeiten anstelle der zwei Zählzeiten im $6/8$-Takt ziemlich jazzig klingen.

Hoedown

Hierbei handelt es sich um einen amerikanischen Square-dance. Die Doppelgriffe mutig angehen, den Bogen dabei auf eine imaginäre „Saite zwischen den Saiten" platzieren. Der synkopierte Rhythmus fällt leicht, wenn man sich zwei Zählzeiten im Takt vorstellt. Beide Spieler können bei den hervorgehobenen Noten in den Takten 10, 12 etc. aufstampfen.